Odd Meter BASSics
By
Dino Monoxelos

Odd Meter BASSics
By Dino Monoxelos

Published by: MonoTunes Music
                           Litchfield NH

About the Author

Originally from the Boston area, Dino Monoxelos has been a professional bass player since he graduated high school (quite some time ago). He's toured with a number of different artists and bands all over the world. He is a graduate of Musicians' Institute and has studied with the likes of Steve Bailey, Gary Willis, Bob Magnusson, Jeff Berlin, Tim Bogert, Jim Lacefield, and Todd Johnson to name just a few. After graduating from MI, Dino began teaching there where he developed his own teaching and playing skills. After seven years of playing and teaching in Los Angeles, Dino has since moved back to his hometown of Boston, MA where he lives with his wife Rachel and daughters Samantha and Nicole. He maintains a very busy playing and teaching schedule as well as being the Senior Product Specialist for Ampeg conducting clinics all over the world!

This book is dedicated to the memory of Jim Lacefield

I would like to thank all of the following people as well.
Mom and Dad and the entire Monoxelos/Sancartier clan, Mom and Dad Doucette & the entire Doucette clan, all the folks at LOUD Technologies/Ampeg, Dana Teague, Michael Brown and everyone at Dana B. Goods, William Bay and everyone at Mel Bay Publications, Mica and Susan Wickersham at Alembic Basses, everyone at Dean Markley Strings, Dave Avenius, Dave Boonshoft, at Aguilar, Frankie A., John and Leo at Lakland Basses, Beaver, Mike and Grasshopper at Bass Central, Dennis, Lee and Dave at The Bass Place, Evan and Chad at Bass Northwest, HP Wilfer at Warwick FZ, my brothers in crime; Dale Titus & Albie Dunbar.

A Very, Very, Very, Special Thanks To:
My wife Rachel for believing in me, and my daughters Samantha and Nicole for teaching me what life is REALLY about. Thank you God for bringing them into my life.

A (Very)Brief History of Odd Meter

So what exactly is Odd Meter? Is it music that is odd or strange? Well to some respect, yes! Odd Meter is basically any music that is written in or contains odd numbered time signatures such as 3/4, 5/4, 7/8, 9/8 etc., the list goes on. Odd meters could be explained as any meter that isn't in 2, 4, or 8. Could a meter of 12/8 be interpreted as an odd meter? Yes and no! It all depends on how it is subdivided. We will get into that in another chapter.

One could write an entire book on the origin of odd meters and their significance in the music of certain cultures. I recommend reading Rhythm & Tempo by Curt Sachs (W.W. Norton & Co. Inc. New York NY). Being raised in a Greek household, I was always exposed to Greek music. Have you ever tried to dance at a Greek wedding? It's hard because most of the traditional Greek songs are either in 5, 7, and sometimes 9/8. There are certain dance steps that are used for this style of music though. This also applies to many Eastern Europe and Middle Eastern cultures. No one is absolutely sure about the origin of odd meters, but it seems to me that it could be dated back to biblical times in the Middle East. It could probably be dated as far back as the first cavemen who banged two rocks together! Who knows? It also applies to some African and South American cultures too.

Odd meter is also used in certain classical pieces. One of the most commonly known piece aside from the traditional 3/4 waltzes was written by Igor Stravinsky in 1913 called The Rite of Spring. Stravinsky was known for his use of changing meters and polyrhythms. Frank Zappa credits Stravinsky as being one of his earliest influences.

When you think of weird or odd music, Frank Zappa definitely has to come to mind as being one of the most popular of contemporary composers. He used odd meters as well as polyrhythms in a large amount of his work.

The progressive rock bands of the seventies and eighties made a career out of writing songs that contained many odd meter changes. Some of the more popular bands like Yes, Emerson, Lake & Palmer, King Crimson, and Rush, turned the rock 'n' roll world on it's ear by incorporating large time signatures and polyrhythms in their compositions. Even pop bands of the nineties are using odd meters in their commercial hits. Artists from Sting to Pearl Jam are all incorporating odd meters in their styles of writing.

Odd meters are used in a lot of the music that we hear today no matter what style of music it is. Whether it's fusion, jazz, rock, pop, or Latin, odd meters play a large part in today's music.

About This Book

As a teacher, I have seen many great books about odd meters that are mostly written by and addressed to drummers. Some of the more popular books on the market today are Odd Time Reading Text by Louis Belleson and Gil Breines, Even In The Odds by Ralph Humphrey, and 2/3 Or Not 2/3 by Efrain Toro. I highly recommend these books in addition to this one though. I have yet to see any books that address odd meters that pertain to bass players though. This book can also be used by other musicians, not just bass players. This book can help anyone get a good grasp of playing in odd meters. You will find however that all the examples are written in bass clef. If you are not familiar with bass clef, don't worry about it. The main thing is to understand the subdivisions of the grooves that pertain to the different styles. Playing along with the CD and following the chord changes with your instrument is all you need to do.

The Intimidation Factor

There is what I have found to be what I call "the intimidation factor" in playing odd meters. Some musicians think that playing in odd meters must mean playing some sort of weird piece of music that has all these strange meter changes in it. Or having to play something that is in say 19/16. That can be true in some cases but for the most part, it can be as simple as playing the bass line to Mission Impossible. Sometimes when doing a T.V. jingle, the composer is given a certain amount of time to fill with music. The entire piece of music could be written in 4/4 time except when we come to the end, there is five seconds of silence, in which case the composer needs to lengthen the piece. This is sometimes done by adding an odd bar somewhere in the piece.

Sometimes odd meters are used to convey certain emotional feelings in songs. A quick tempo 5/8 can convey the feeling of confusion or disarray. Believe it or not but a slow tempo, 7/8 samba can be very relaxing.

Playing in odd meters should come as naturally to the musician as playing in 4/4. One other misconception that I see quite often is when a student comes to me and plays something in let's say 13/8, and tells me how he or she spent days trying to figure something out in 13/8. The whole idea is to not "try" to figure anything out. If a groove comes naturally to you and it happens to be in an odd meter, GREAT. Then it's easy to play, right! If you have to sit down and figure something out, it could take days before it comes naturally. That's perfectly okay too! What I'm saying is, don't write something in an odd meter just for the sake of it being in an odd meter, unless of course you're the poor composer that we talked about before. Some people spend months composing a piece of music with all these strange time changes in it just for the sake of it being in odd meters, and the end result isn't always music. Here's something that you can try. Experiment playing with grooves in different meters, but record yourself while doing this. Then go back to the recording and hear what you just played and then figure out what time it's in. I always have students coming to my class with an idea in his or her head but they can't figure out what time it's in. They will play it for me while I record it and then we'll both sit down and figure out what time it's in. At least in this case the idea feels so natural to them that they have no problem remembering it!

Explanation of a Time Signature

For those of you who aren't familiar with what a time signature means, here's a brief explanation. Let's take a 4/4 time signature for example. The top number will always tell us how many beats to a measure. In this case we have four beats to a measure. The bottom number will always tell us which type of note value receives one beat. In this case the bottom number four tells us that the quarter note will receive one beat each. Now, let's look at a 7/8 time signature! The top number, in this case, seven, tells us that there are seven beats to each measure. The bottom number, eight, tells us that the eighth note will receive one beat each. Whenever you hear someone refer to "a bar of seven" or "a bar of 9" or "this chart is in 5", they are referring to the top number in the time signature. Whether the quarter note or the eighth note receives the beat depends on the overall feel of the song. We will discuss this subject in another chapter.

Explanation of the 2 - 3 Subdivision

All meters, even the most common meters are simply combinations of twos and threes. Just as computer code is nothing more that ones and zeros, the same stands true for any type of meter. Let's take a bar of 5/8 for example. Remember, five beats per measure, and the eighth note receives the beat. Example 1a. shows us what a simple bar of 5/8 looks like. Now look at example 1b., notice how it is subdivided into a section of two eighth notes and then a section of three eighth notes.

This is a common subdivision of 5/8. We'll call this a 2 - 3 subdivision. Notice the accent markings above each grouping. Now, set your metronome up to 80 bpm, each click on the metronome will represent one eighth note. The eighth note is the largest common denominator for this particular meter. First clap example 1a. Without using the accents, it's hard to determine where the bar starts and stops without having to count.

Now try clapping example 1b. accenting each group. I want you to tap with both hands alternating, on your chest, or your lap, the 8th notes, in the sub-divisions that we put them in, accenting each group....slowly!   Notice that if you lead with your right hand on the first time, the second time then makes you lead with your left hand and visa-versa. Try doing this first leading with your right hand then your left. This may seem awkward at first but it'll come to you with practice. These are basic rudiments that drummers practice all the time. If it's too fast, feel free to slow the tempo on your metronome. I know by now you're probably asking why are there drum exercises in a bass book. Trust me, this will improve your feel of the groove no matter what meter you are in and whatever instrument you play.

Now let's look at example 1c. Nothing has changed as far as the time signature and the subdivision. What we did was combine the first group of two eighth notes into a quarter note, and the second group of three eighth notes into a dotted quarter note. Try clapping example 1c. with the metronome clicking off the five eighth notes. Again, if it's too fast or too complicated at first, turn the metronome slower or even turn it off until you feel comfortable playing these exercises.

Now look at example 1d. Again nothing has been done to the time signature or the subdivisions. What we did was take the first group of two eighth notes and break them down into sixteenth notes. The last group of three eighth notes we broke down into six sixteenth notes. Instead of having a group of four sixteenth notes and a group of two sixteenth notes, we simply split them into two equal groups of three sixteenth notes. Try clapping this using two hands on your lap or chest.

In example 1e, we now have two dotted eighth notes in the second grouping instead of a dotted quarter note like we had in example 1c. Here's your workout for this chapter....

Be able to clap examples 1b and 1d while tapping either example 1c, or 1e with your foot. Be able to alternate between all four combinations without stopping. Like I said earlier, if the metronome gets to be too confusing, turn it off at first and work out the coordination between your hands and your feet. Start this and all the following exercise slow at first! You don't want to create any bad habits!!

2 - 3 Subdivision

The Clap! How To Use This Book

You will notice that throughout this book I'm always saying to clap out the exercises on your lap or chest before you pick up your bass and play them. This is probably the most important thing that you can do. DO NOT play these exercises without being able to clap them out first. Each time signature is broken down into two sections, The Examples, and The Ideas. You must be able to tap out the exercises on your lap or better yet, a drum of some sort, before you can move on to playing the ideas on you bass! If you go straight to the ideas without working on the examples, the whole purpose of this book will be lost.

One thing I've noticed is that when I show a student a groove in any odd meter, they don't have a problem repeating what I just played...sorta! The problem comes when they have to play the groove on their own, without any accompaniment. What happens is we start to guess where the beat is instead of actually knowing it. This can get pretty hairy especially when you're playing with a drummer who likes to play things over the bar line. I see a lot of students who when they first try to work out a new rhythm, they attempt to play it on their bass first. Next thing you know, they're guessing the rhythm instead of knowing it. Put the bass away! Try to clap out the rhythm first. If you have a hard time trying to clap the rhythm, what makes you think that playing it on the bass will make it any easier. Remember, if you can't clap it, you can't play it. The rhythm has to come from within. By clapping out these rhythms, you are internalizing everything in this book. Wouldn't you rather be able to feel 5/8 instead of having to count it out every time you play. I'll bet you my entire pet rock collection that when you play a funk line, you don't have to actually count 1+2+3+4+. Of course you don't, that's because you are so used to playing and being exposed to that type of meter, that it has become internal. That's what you are doing with all these odd meters, internalizing them. You can go through this entire book without an instrument. All you need is a good sense of time and your own two hands, THAT'S IT! Some of these exercises may require some very simple hand/foot coordination. Like I said before, if you can play a funk line and tap your foot to 4/4 time at the same time, you'll have no problems with this book. One last thing to remember, as bass players, chances are you will be playing some of the more simplified rhythms as ostinatos. This doesn't mean that the sixteenth note exercises aren't important though. You must be able to feel the sixteenth note in order to play any style or meter. I can't stress that enough to my students. The greatest players in the world all have that one thing in common. Even if they're playing a simple quarter note groove, they're still feeling that sixteenth note pulse. In the examples, you'll usually se□¡e the groove broken down into sixteenth notes first and then just below that example, you'll see the ostinato. The ostinato is what you will actually be playing on the bass.

Good Luck with this book. I truly hope that it will shed some light on playing in odd meters!

Explanation On Using The Exercises, Ideas, and then Charts

You will notice that for each time signature there are three different sections, The Exercises, The Ideas, and then The Charts. The book is set up so that you can go from one section right to the next, within one specific time signature.

The Exercises are designed to show you how each time signature can be broken down into different subdivisions. When going through these exercises, all that you should be doing is clapping exercises to familiarize or internalize each subdivision. When you've accomplished that, you can then move on to The Ideas.

The Ideas are set up to demonstrate different types of grooves that can be played on your bass. Just about all of these ideas are derived from the different subdivisions that you just practiced from The Exercises section. Once this is done, you can then move on to The Charts.

The Charts are basic blues progressions, I-IV-V's. I stuck with a basic chord progression to keep it simple. Remember, it's not your knowledge of chord structures that we are working on here. It's how well you can play each time signature through a basic chord chart. Pay close attention to the subdivision in the first bar of each chart. This tells you what type of subdivision is being used throughout the chart. When you've mastered that, try using your own subdivisions by playing along with a drummer or drum machine.

The last section of the book includes a few charts for those of you that just can't get enough. These are some multi-meter charts that you can play along with the cd or with your own band. Pay close attention to the time changes and their respective subdivisions.

3/4 & 3/8

I wanted to start with 3/4 & 3/8 for a couple of reasons. First, 3/4 and 3/8 are the most common types of odd meters along with 6/4, 6/8 and 12/8. Mainly because they contain groupings of only three at a time. Second, most forms of three are used in the traditional waltzes and jazz swing patterns. These of which we are probably all familiar with. Third, like I said earlier, all odd meters are combinations of 2's and 3's. Well we all know how to play in 2 right? Remember 4/4 is a combination of a 2 + 2 subdivision. When we get to three though, everyone seems to think that playing three quarter notes or three eighth notes, is all there is to playing in three. Au Contraire! There is so much more to it than that. How about playing "two" OVER "three". This is called a polyrythm, when one meter is superimposed over another or, in other words, when one meter is played in the same space as another meter. This is essential to learn because every odd meter that contains a "three" subdivision, now you can superimpose a "two" feel over the "three" section of the meter.

Here are a few songs that come to mind when I think of songs in 3/4 and 3/8. Be sure to check them out.

All Blues - Miles Davis
Footprints - Wayne Shorter
Manic Depression - Jimi Hendrix
My Favorite Things - R. Rodgers

3/4 Examples

Let's set up a metronome or a drum machine. Set the tempo to approximately 80bpm. Remember that the click is the largest common denominator. In 3/4 it will click as the quarter note and in 3/8 it will click as the eighth note. Experiment with the tempo so that you can work on these exercises slowly at first. If it gets to be too much go ahead and turn the metronome off until you feel comfortable.

Let's look at example 2a. This is a common bar of 3/4. It looks pretty straight ahead right, three quarter notes to a bar. Now break the quarter notes down to eighth notes and you have example 2b. Try to play example 2a with your foot while tapping out example 2b with your hands. Pretty straight forward right? Now, while still playing example 2a with your foot, move down to example 2c with your hands. This might be a little more difficult. Remember to follow the accents. Continue tapping down to example 2g while keeping example 2a in your foot. Example 2d is a perfect example of a 2 over 3 polyrhythm. You are fitting two equal notes over three beats. Example 2g is another example of a polyrhythm. You are fitting four equal notes over three beats giving us a four over three polyrhythm. Polyrhythms great to work on because give the time signature a whole new feel to it. Hence if you are playing 2 over 3. You are implying a 2 feel in a 3/4 time signature. If you have trouble with example 2f and 2g, try clapping 2f first while playing 2g with your foot. It's very important that you get those dotted eighth notes and dotted quarter notes feeling real comfortable.

3/4 Examples

3/4 Ideas

#11

Am

Funk

#12

#13

#14

3/4 Ideas

Here are some bass lines based on the 3/4 examples that you can work on. Remember, you have to be able to clap the examples first before you pick up your bass to try these ideas. You'll find that a lot of the sixteenth note exercise that we practice might be a little too busy to play on the bass. It is still very important to practice them. Even though you're not playing the sixteenth notes, it's very important that you are feeling them. IN ANY TIME SIGNATURE. You'll also notice that some of these ideas can be played in a number of different styles, not just the one specified above the idea. Be sure to experiment with these ideas, you may be surprised with what you come up with. Play each idea all the way through without stopping and don't forget about the repeats. Try playing these ideas with the CD.
The first 4 ideas are based off of a waltz. They are pretty straight forward. Each idea is just has just a little more added to it from the previous idea.

The next 3 ideas (#5, #6, #7) are just 3/4 swing. The main idea here is to feel the "three" in a swing. Most of us are real comfortable swinging in "four". Here's where it's real important to feel the "three". The next four ideas are all based off of a rock feel. Keep in mind though that they will also work in other styles as well, such as swing. Ideas #8 and #9 are great to see how some of these polyrhythms work. The 4 over 3 works well as a turn around at the end of a four bar phrase like in #8. Ideas 12, 13 and 14 are proof that you can get funky in 3/4. There is nothing special about it. The rhythms are straight forward. It's just the way that they are played that makes the difference. They could be used as rock ideas.

3/8 Examples

Let's take a look at the 3/8 examples now. You'll notice that some of these examples are very similar to the 3/4 examples. There is a difference between the two time signatures though. 3/8 is used more commonly for swing style patterns. You can think of 3/8 as sort of a double time 3/4 for now but as we get further in to changing meters, you will see the difference.

Okay, let's get started. Let's set up a metronome or drum machine. Set the tempo to 100 bpm. The click will now be our eighth note because the eighth note is the largest common denominator in this meter. Example 3a is as easy as it gets. Three eighth notes to a measure representing the 3/8 time signature. If you tie all three eighth notes together, you have what we see in example 3b, a dotted quarter note. Now, break down each eighth note into sixteenth notes and we have three groups of two sixteenth notes each. By grouping
the sixteenth notes into three we have example 3d. If you tie each group of three sixteenth notes together, we come up with two dotted eighth notes. Again, here is another form of a 2 over 3 polyrhythm, two dotted eighth notes over a bar of 3/8, giving us a "two" feel. Example 3f would work well using it as a turn around at the end of a two or four bar phrase.
Be able to tap all these rhythms with your hands while tapping example 3a with your foot.

3/8 Examples

3a

3b

3c

3d

3e

3f

3/8 Ideas

3/8 Ideas cont.

#5

#6

#7 | Funk |

3/8 Ideas

Here are some 3/8 ideas that you can work on. Remember, you must have the 3/8 clapping exercises down before you can move on to these ideas. Notice how the ideas in this section are all eight bar phrases instead of the previous four bar phrases. Idea #1 is just a 3/8 swing pattern over a common II-V-I chord progression. Idea #2 is the same progression only we are now using the 2 over 3 polyrhythm to give it more of a "two" feel. Idea #3 is still a swing pattern but you are implying a waltz feel just by adding that fast eighth note on beat three. The next three ideas are some basic rock grooves that are adapted to fit the 3/8 time signature. Notice how example 3f works nice as a turn around at the end of some of these phrases. Remember that these rock ideas will work well as swing ideas too, especially the turn around in example 3f. It's all in how you play them. Idea #7 is yet another proof that you can play funk in 3/8 too. These funk ideas could work well in a swing feel and a rock feel too. Again, it's all in how you play them. Be sure to experiment with these ideas in different styles.

3/4 & 3/8 Chart

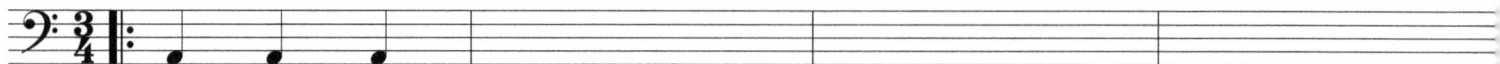

Am

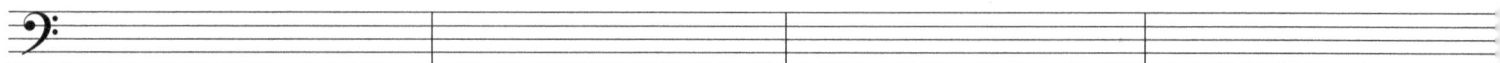

Dm   Am

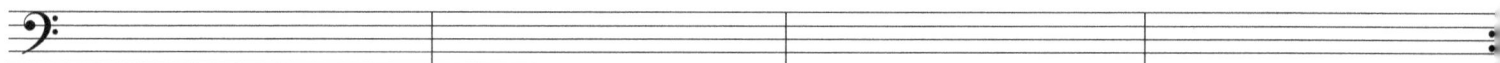

E⁷   D⁷   Am

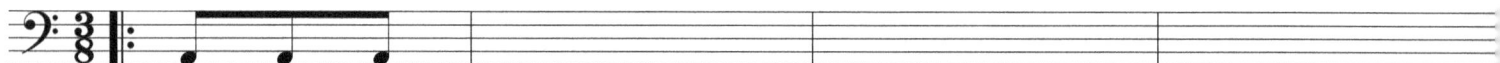

Am

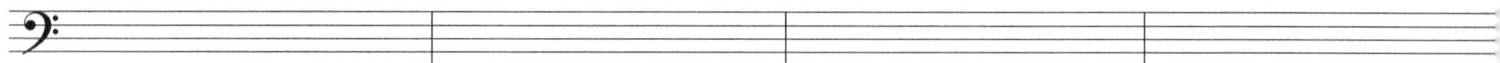

Dm

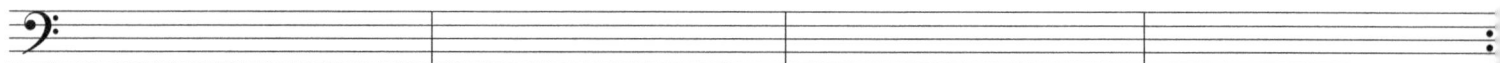

E⁷   D⁷   Am

This page intentionally left blank to facilitate page turns......

6/4 & 6/8

Now that you've got 3/4 and 3/8 mastered let's move on to some more familiar meters. In this next section we'll look at 6/4 and 6/8. We will be using a 3 - 3 subdivision for most of these 6/4 and 6/8 ideas. You're probably thinking "well can't I just combine two 3/4's to make a 6/4 and two 3/8's to make 6/8?" The answer to that is yes and no. You can combine the two but, it gets far more interesting when you start to subdivide 6/4 and 6/8. 6/4 and 6/8 are most commonly used in gospel, blues, and some R&B styles, unlike 3/4 and 3/8 which are use in swing and waltzes. Again, that doesn't limit us to only those particular styles. Remember, learn the meter, then incorporate it into your style of playing whether it be rock, funk, jazz etc.

6/4 Examples

Let's set up a metronome or a drum machine. Set the tempo to approximately 80bpm. Remember the click is the largest common denominator for whatever time you are in. In 6/4 it's the quarter note. Experiment with the tempo at first so that you can work on these exercises slowly. If the metronome is too much at first, turn it off until you feel comfortable playing these exercises.

Let's take a look at some 6/4 exercises. Remember you must practice these exercises before you can move on to the playing ideas.
Example 4a is pretty straight forward...six quarter notes to a measure. If we break the six quarter notes down into eighth notes we have example 4b. Now, we take those eighth notes and group them into four groups of three. This gives us example 4c. Let's take each group of three eighth notes and tie them together. This gives us four dotted quarter notes like in example 4d. Now we have four dotted eighth notes over six beats, (4 over 6). Let's go back to example 4c, instead of grouping the eighth notes into groups of three, let's group them into two groups of three, and three groups of two. This is what we have in example 4e. Now let's take the last three groups of two and combine them into three quarter notes, example 4f. Now take the two groups of three and combine them into two dotted quarter notes, this will give us example 4g. Now let's go back to example 4a. Instead of breaking the quarter notes down into eighth notes, this time we'll break them down in to sixteenth notes like in example 4h. Example 4i gives us a different twist by grouping the sixteenth notes into four groups of three and three groups of four. If we combine them all together into their largest common denominator, we have example 4j. Practice tapping all of these exercises from 4a down to 4j while tapping 4a with your foot. This will give you different ideas to play over 6/4. Don't forget about the accent markings, these are very important to accent each grouping. Does 4d, 4e, and 4f sound familiar? If you've ever seen West Side Story then it should. Remember, do these slowly at first and when you fell comfortable with them, move on to the ideas.

6/4 Examples

4a

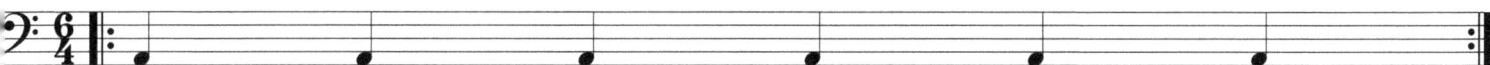

4b

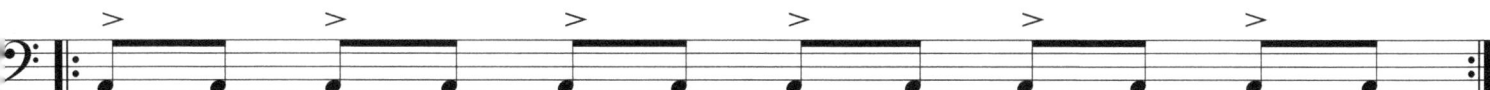

4c

4d

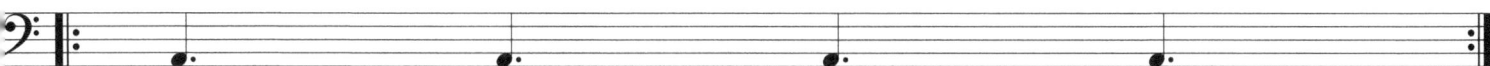

4e

4f

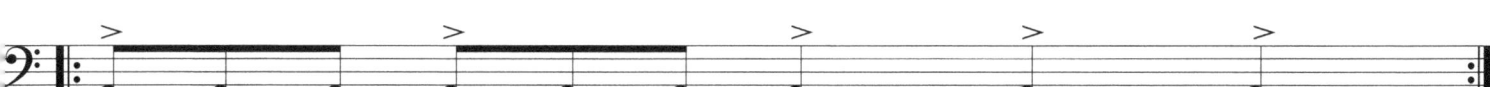

4g

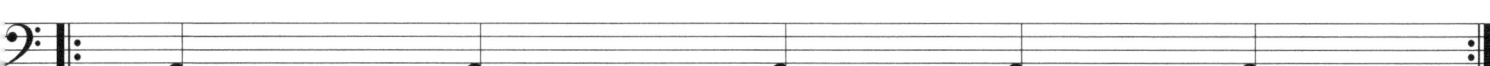

4h

4i

4j

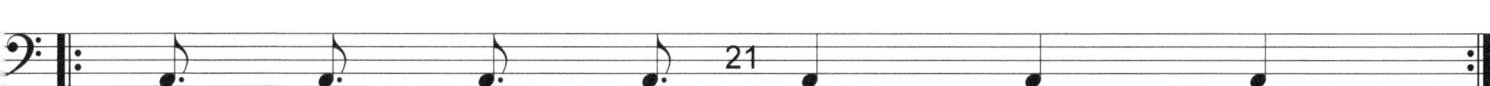

6/4 Ideas

6/4 Ideas cont.

Rock

/4 Ideas

Now that you've mastered the examples, let's move on to playing some of these ideas. Ideas #1, #2 and 3 are some basic swing ideas that can be used over a II-V-I progression. Just a simple walking line with the quarter note. Each idea has something different added to it though. Try combining these ideas nd come up with your own walking line. Be sure to swing those eighth notes! Ideas #4 and #5 can be sed as a gospel feel. Again, be sure to swing those eighth notes. Ideas #7, #8 and #9 can all be used s a Latin feel over 6/4 due to the root - fifth construction. Remember, these ideas will work well with whatever style you want. These ideas are just suggestions. Ideas #9, #10, and #11 are some basic rock grooves that will work well too. Idea #9 is written two different ways. The second way makes it easier to ee the subdivisions. Try all these ideas in whatever style you choose. Be sure to practice them slowly t first and gradually build up the tempo.

6/8 Examples

Let's move on to 6/8. Like 3/4 and 3/8, there will be some similarities between 6/8 and 6/4. You will also see a lot of similarities between 6/8 and 3/4. Remember, 3/4 has six, eighth notes to a measure too. The overall "feel" of the two meters are completely different though. Look at example 5a. Again, very straight forward. Six eighth notes to a measure. If you combine the eighth notes together though, you get example 5b which is a bar of 3/4. Here is where the similarities end. Take the eighth note in example 5a and group them into two groups of three like in example 5c. If we take those eighth notes and tie them into dotted quarter notes, we have example 5d which is a 2 over 6 polyrhythm. Now let's move on to sixteenth notes. If we break the six eighth notes down into sixteenth notes, that will give us twelve sixteenth notes. Group the sixteenth notes into four groups of three and we have example 5e. Example 5f shows □us what we would come up with by combining each group of three sixteenth notes together, four dotted eighth notes over six beats (4 over 6). It sounds complicated but if you look closely, it's really just 2 over 3, done twice within the bar. Now let's group the sixteenth notes into two groups of three, a group of four, and then a group of two (example 5g). Combine each group into its largest common denominator and we have example 5h. Look at example 5i, it is basically just like example 5g except notice the accents on the last three groups of sixteenth notes. Just adding one more subdivision changes the whole feel at the end of the bar. Example 5j is what we come up with by combining each group into it's largest common denominator. Examples 5h and 5j give us that 2 over 3 feel in the first half of the bar.

Be sure to practice tapping all these examples from 5a down to 5j while tapping 5a with your foot. Start off slow and then bump the tempo up when you get comfortable with them. If you feel real daring, try tapping these examples while tapping 5b, and then 5d with you foot. GOOD LUCK!

6/8 Examples

5a

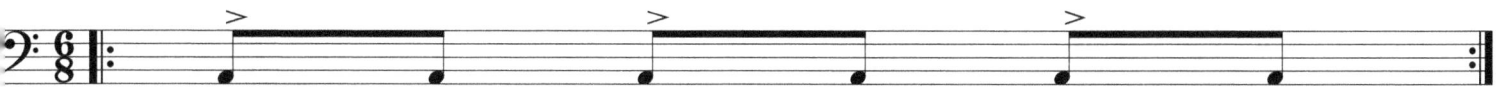

5b

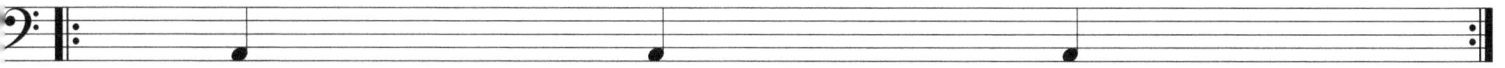

5c

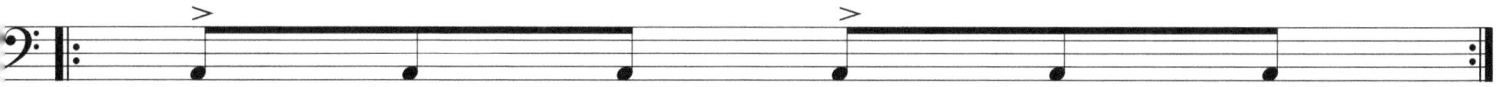

5d

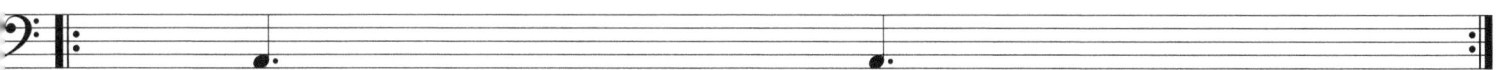

5e

5f

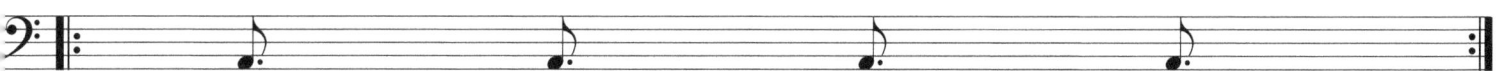

5g

5h

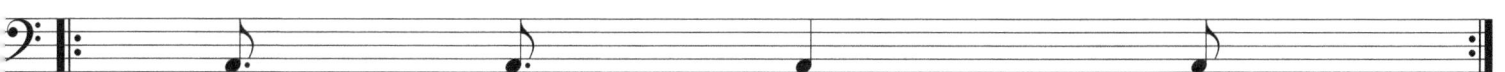

5i

5j

25

6/8 Ideas

#1 Am⁷   D⁷   Gmaj⁷   ℅

#2 Am⁷   D⁷   Gmaj⁷   ℅

#3 Am⁷   D⁷   Gmaj⁷   ℅

#4

#5

#6

#7

#8

#9

26

#10

#11

#12

6/8 Ideas

Okay, now that you have the 6/8 ideas under your hands, let's move on to the ideas. Most of these ideas are based off of the examples. You will notice a couple that aren't based off of the examples. They are based off of the sixteenth note though, so if you did your homework, you won't have any problems with them. Okay, let's get started!

The first three ideas are just a few ways to play a walking line over 6/8. Idea #1 is just a simple eighth note walking line over a II-V-I chord progression. Idea #2 gives us a 2 over 3 walking line with the same chord progression. This works real good as a turn around at the end of a phrase. Idea #3 will give you a two feel over the same progression. Try doing these ideas over any chord progression. If you're out of ideas, open up a real book and try them over your favorite standards. Ideas #4 - #9 can work with just about any type of style. They were primarily done as either a rock or a funk style but will work over anything. Try playing them over different progressions. I think you'll be surprised. Ideas #4 and #5 start each bar with the 2 over 3 feel and then complete the bar with either three eighth notes or the quarter note, eighth note figure like in #5. Ideas #8 and #9 are pretty much the same except for #9 has more of a staccato sound to it due to the sixteenth note rests separating the upbeats. Ideas # 9 and #10 have a sort of Samba feel to them so they would work well over certain Latin styles. Ideas #12 is a basic walking blues line. It would work over any type of 12 bar blues.

Remember, practice these ideas slowly at first and then as you get comfortable with them, bump up the tempo. Have fun.

6/4 & 6/8 Chart

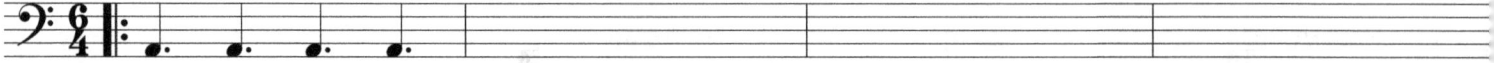

Am

Dm   Am

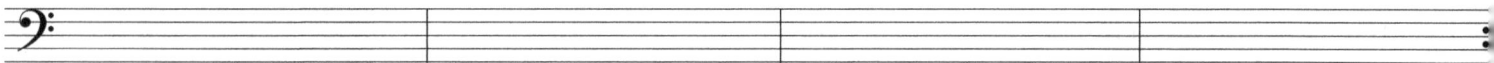

E⁷   D⁷   Am

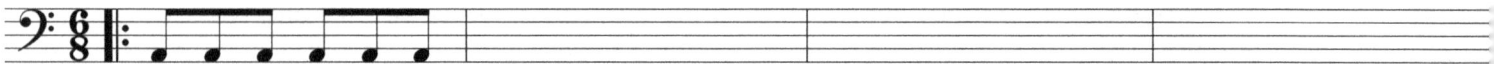

Am

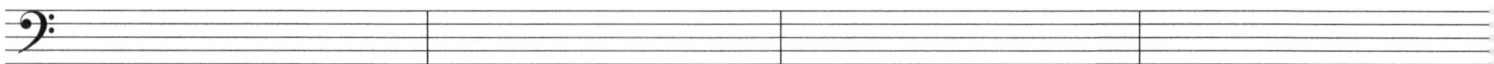

Dm

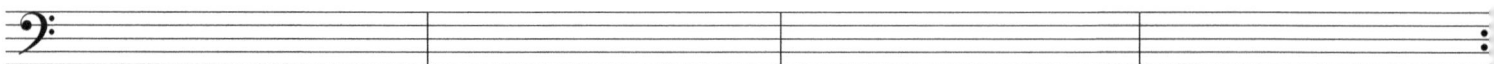

E⁷   D⁷   Am

12/8

12/8 is probably the most common of all the triple meters. Mainly because it is used in a wide majority of rock, rhythm & blues, blues, and jazz styles. The most common is what we know as a blues shuffle and a slow blues. Again, learn all the following exercises and then incorporate them into your style of playing.

12/8 Examples

Let's get started. Example 6a is the first and the most common subdivision for 12/8. Four groups of three eighth notes. Essentially we could turn those eighth notes into eighth note triplets and then we would be in 4/4. Hhhhmmm, something to think about. Okay, let's look at 6b. By replacing the middle eighth note with an eighth note rest, we have the basics of a shuffle. By grouping each group of eighth notes together, we have the dotted quarter note like in example 6c. Examples 6d, 6e, 6f and 6g are all combinations of 6a, 6b, and 6c. All these examples so far have been in groupings of three, so they still have a triplet or triple feel to them. Example 6h - 6l combine the tr□iplet feel with a duple feel. Example 6i is four groups of four sixteenth notes followed by two groups of three sixteenth notes, followed by a group of two sixteenth notes. Example 6j is the ostinato based off of example 6i. Look very closely at example 6j. What other combination of time signatures could that be considered? If you said a bar of 4/4 and a bar of 2/4, you're right. One thing that you'll notice is the fact that there are a few different ways to write out different time signatures. The one thing that will never change is the way that they're played though. It's all in how YOU play them!

Remember don't forget about the accents for each group. Do these examples slowly at first until they feel comfortable. We're not trying to win any races. Here's a pointer for you. Even though in some examples you play notes as long as a dotted quarter, you should still be feeling the eighth note pulse.

12/8 Examples

6a

6b

6c

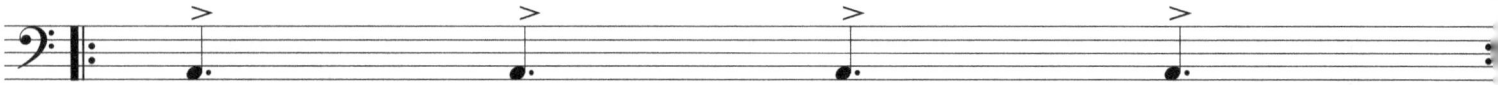

6d

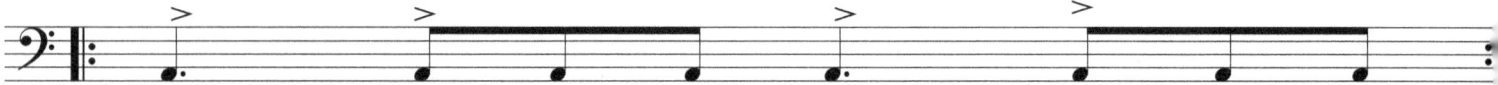

6e

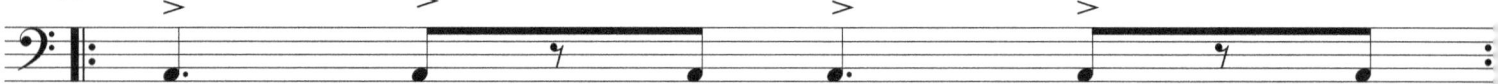

6f

6g

6h

6i

6j

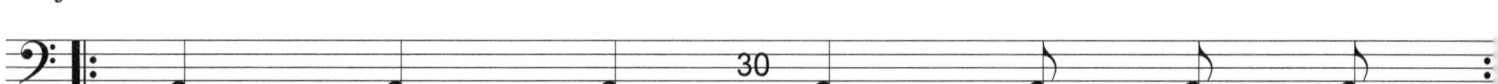

6k

6l

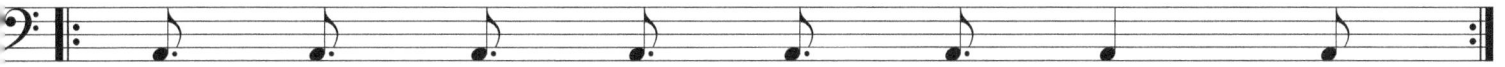

12/8 Ideas

Let's move on to some 12/8 ideas. You will notice some pretty common 12/8 ideas here. You'll also notice some not so common but nonetheless easy 12/8 ideas too. Ideas #1 - #6 are pretty straight ahead blues ideas. If you plan on sitting in on a jam session any time, these are a few ideas that might save your life on a blues gig. Idea #1 is a basic Chicago shuffle pattern (root, octave, m7, 5). Idea #2 is the same pattern but notice the eighth note rests in the middle of each group of three. Be sure pay attention to those rests, they give the idea a whole new feel. Try alternating between #1 and #2. Ideas #4 and #5 are the same way. They are identical patterns but the rests give #5 a different feel, almost a more staccato feel. Idea #3 is a pattern that works very well over a slow blues where the drummer will actually play all twelve eighth notes on the high hat or ride cymbal. Idea #6 is a variation of #4, just a straight ahead walking blues line without the shuffle feel. It has more of a straight walking line. Be careful of the triplet figure at the end of the bar though. Idea #7 has sort of a 1950s doo-wap feel to it. That would also work well over a slow blues too. Ideas #8 and #9 are based off of 6 and 7 but they have more of a straight feel to them. Be careful of those dotted eighth notes in #9. Idea #10 has more of a funky feel to it than the others. This isn't something you would see everyday in 12/8 but it sounds cool. It would work well as a turn around too. Idea #11 is another type of walking line but the two dotted eighth note followed by a single eighth note give the idea a completely different feel. This would work well as a funk or as a rock groove. Idea #12 is an ostinato based off of example 6I. Make sure you are giving each dotted eighth note it's full value. This is where all that tapping will pay off. Ideas #13 and #14 have a Latin fell to them. Idea #13 will work well as a 12/8 bossa nova and #14 will work as a samba.

Practice these ideas slow at first and remember, these ideas are only suggestions of the examples. Feel free to experiment with your own examples and ideas and incorporate them into your own playing style.

12/8 Ideas

#11   G⁷

#12   Gm

#13

#14

12/8 Chart

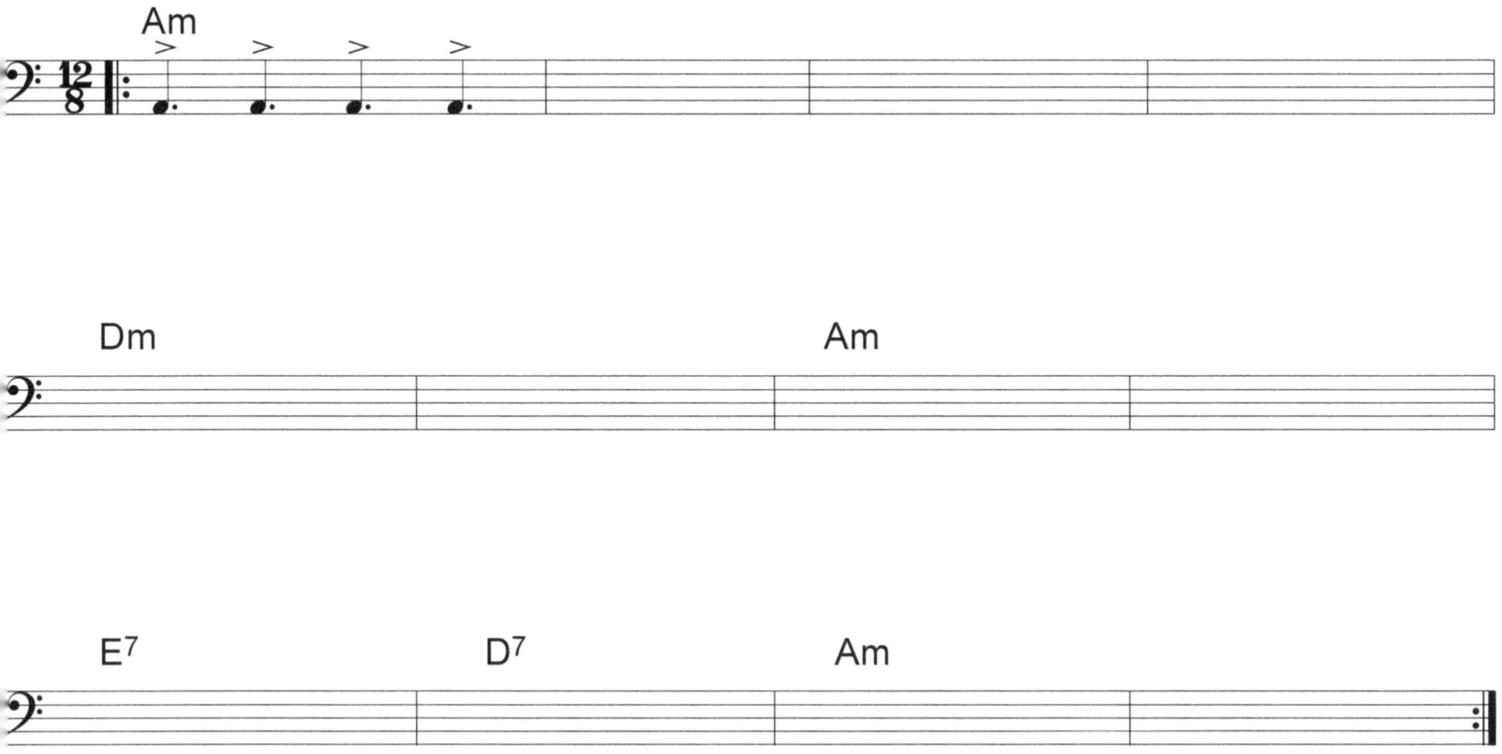

5/8 and 5/4

5/8 and 5/4 are the next two meters that I would like to talk about. Playing in 5 gets us a little more into what everyone considers to be "odd meter". The previous chapters that dealt with triples are more common to us because they have more of a common swing or shuffle feel. 5/8 and 5/4 will seem to have more of a "skip" feel to it meaning it will feel like you are skipping a beat. 5/8 and 5/4 will usually be broken down in to a 3-2 subdivision. Sometimes you will see it as a 2-3 subdivision too. Among these subdivisions you will also have smaller subdivisions. I will explain these when we get to them. A few songs that come to mind are the theme from "Mission Impossible" (5/8), David Brubeck's "Take Five" (5/4). Led Zeppelin fans will remember songs like "The Crunge" (5/4) and "Four Sticks" (5/8).

5/4 Examples

Let's set up a metronome or a drum machine. Set the tempo to approximately 80bpm. Remember the click is the largest common denominator for whatever time you are in. In 5/4 it's the quarter note. Experiment with the tempo at first so that you can work on these exercises slowly. If the metronome is too much at first, turn it off until you feel comfortable playing these exercises.

Let's start with example 7a. It looks pretty straight forward right? Notice how the accents are placed above the quarter notes. The first accent is placed above the first quarter note but the second accent is placed above the fourth quarter. By doing this we have what we call a 3+2 subdivision. Each click on the metronome is a quarter note so make sure you accent beats one and four. Example 7b is what happens when you tie each group of quarter notes together. Let's break the quarter notes into eighth notes. This is what we see in example 7c. The only difference is that I subdivided the eighth notes into two groups of three and two groups of 2 (3+3+2+2). By doing this, it will give us a 2 over 3 feel in the first half of the bar. Keep in mind though that we are still in a 3+2 subdivision. Example 7d is what we come up with by tying each group of eighth notes together (two dotted quarter notes, and two quarter notes).

Examples 7e - 7h are all based on a slower tempo do to the fact that they are all derived from the sixteenth note subdivisions. Example 7e is just five groups of four quarter notes. Examples 7f, 7g, and 7h are all based off of example 7d. All we did was take the dotted quarter notes and subdivide them in half. Example 7f is four groups of three sixteenth notes and two groups of four sixteenth notes. Example 7g and 7h are the ostinatos we come up with based off of example 7f. It is very important that you can play the groups of three in 7f. This is very important otherwise you won't be able to feel those dotted eighth notes in examples 7g and 7h

Try clapping all of these examples from 7a all the way down to 7h while keeping 7a in your foot. When you get to the sixteenth note subdivisions, you will probably need to slow the tempo to allow for the sixteenth notes groupings. Try all these examples at different speeds as an experiment.

5/4 Examples

5/4 Ideas

#1   Dm

#2   Dm

#3   Amaj⁷   F♯m⁷   Bm⁷   E⁷

#4   E⁷

#5   Am

#6   Am

#7   A⁷

#8   Am

#9   Am

#10   Amaj⁷   F♯m⁷   Bm⁷   E⁷

38

Bonus Idea (try to guess the song!)

5/4 Ideas

Okay, let's take a look at some of the following 5/4 ideas. Ideas #1 and #2 are both based off of the 3+2 eighth note subdivision. Idea #1 is a sample of the bass line from Dave Brubeck's "Take 5", and idea #2 is the bass line from "Mission Impossible" and is another example of playing 2 over 3 in the group of three subdivision. Idea #3 is a weird one, the subdivision alternates between bars. The first bar has a 3+2 subdivision, while the second bar has a 2+3 subdivision. Idea #4 is a funk line that has a 3+2 subdivision. It's hard to tell, but the two groups of eighth notes at the end of the bar is the giveaway. Remember, some subdivisions aren't as blatant as others! Any Led Zeppelin fans? Idea #5 should sound familiar. It's based off of a 2+3 subdivision. Ideas #6, #7, #8 and #9 are all based off the sixteenth note so this means you might want to slow the metronome down to a reasonable tempo. If you worked on the 5/8 examples then these dotted eighth notes should come fairly simple. If not, then you're really only guessing where each dotted eighth notes falls. It's real important that you give each dotted eighth note it's full value. Ideas #8 and #9 are identical. #9 is just a little more syncopated. Idea #10 is the bonus idea. If you can get that down you are well on your way. It's basically a 4/4 groove with an added beat. Yes, sometimes the most obvious solutions are the hardest.
All these ideas work very well over a number of different styles. That's why I didn't categorize them this time. Experiment for yourself and see what you can come up with. Remember to start off slow at first and....well you get the idea!

Good Luck with the bonus idea. It really doesn't have much of a subdivision. It's pretty much just five straight beats to a bar but it's fun to play. Besides, I don't think the guy who wrote it was too concerned about subdivisions. Like I said in the very beginning of this book, if a groove or an idea comes naturally to you, who cares what the subdivision is, you can always record yourself and then figure out the subdivisions later. The main thing is that it grooves and it feels comfortable

5/8 Examples

Now let's move on to some 5/8 examples. Let's set up a metronome or a drum machine. Set the tempo to approximately 80bpm. Remember the click is the largest common denominator for whatever time you are in. In 5/8 it's the eighth note. Experiment ☐with the tempo at first so that you can work on these exercises slowly. If the metronome is too much at first, turn it off until you feel comfortable playing these exercises.

You will notice some similarities between 5/8 and 5/4 as far as subdivisions go. Remember though, 5/4 and 5/8 are two completely different meters. 5/8 is a relatively small meter (5 eighth notes to a measure). Whereas 5/4 has 5 quarter notes to a measure.

Okay, let's get started! Example 8a is a 3+2 subdivision of 5/8, one of the most common. In fact, there really are only two logical ways to subdivided 5/8, 3+2, or 2+3. Anyway, for right now we'll stick with 3+2. If we subdivide the eighth notes into sixteenth notes, we have example 8b. Notice the subdivision for 8b, 3+3+2+2. We are still in a 3+2 subdivision of 5/8, we are now subdividing within a subdivision. By combining the groups of sixteenth notes, we have the ostinato shown in examples 8c, 8d, and 8e. The two dotted eighth notes in the beginning of the measure emphasize once again the 2 over 3 feel. Again, this is where all those sixteenth note rhythms come into play.

We are going to try practicing something a little different with these examples though. Instead of having to frantically tap your foot to 5 eighth notes per measure, try tapping example 8e with your foot while tapping 8a - 8e with your hands. When you get to example 8f notice that the subdivisions are flipped around. We are now in a 2+3 subdivision. All the examples are the same except that they are all flipped flopped. Practice tapping examples 8f - 8j with your hands while tapping 8j with your foot. Don't forget about all those accents too. One thing to beware of; make sure to give the downbeat of each measure a little heavier accent. Sometimes the subdivision can get flipped from 3+2 to 2+3 without you even noticing it.

5/8 Examples

5/8 Ideas

Now that we have looked at two of the more common subdivisions of 5/8, let's move on to the ideas. All of these ideas are based on either a 3+2 subdivision or the 2+3 subdivision like we practiced in the examples.

Idea # 1 is the basic two dotted eighth notes followed by two eighth notes. Make sure to give those dotted eighth notes their full value to get that 2 over 3 feel. Idea #2 is more of the same only it's more in the vein of "Mission Impossible". Idea #3 is a more subdivided version of #2. The only difference is that the second dotted eighth note is divided into an eighth note - sixteenth note figure. Idea #4 could be used as a Latin groove over 5/8, this is due to the notes being used though (root-fifth-octave). You can use this idea over many other types of styles though. Remember, even though you're only playing a dotted eighth note in the beginning of the bar, you should still feel those dotted eighth notes even though you're not playing them. The same goes for idea #5. This idea is as basic as it gets. The thing that will make it work though is that you must be able to feel all the subdivisions even though you're not playing them. That's what will make this groove.

Ideas #6, #7, #8, and #9 are all based off of a 2+3 subdivision. Just like in the examples, be careful not to flip-flop the subdivisions around. This is real easy to due by mistake. Look at idea #8 for example. It's identical to idea #1 right? The only difference is that #8 starts with two eighth notes followed by two dotted eighth notes. Just the opposites of #1. Sound familiar? If you're a Led Zeppelin fan then it should, ("Four Sticks"). If we were to draw an imaginary bar line down the center of first and second measures, the figure between those imaginary bar lines would be what we see in idea #1. The same also goes for idea #9 and idea #5! So this goes to prove that it's all in how you play each idea. Be sure to give the down beat of each bar a little heavier accent to be sure.

5/8 Ideas

#1

#2

#3

#4

#5

#6

#7

#8

#9

5/4 & 5/8 Chart

This page intentionally left blank to facilitate page turns......

7/4 and 7/8

7/4 and 7/8 are the next two time signatures that we'll look at. There are many styles that these two meter can be used effectively in. Next to playing in five, seven is the second most commonly used odd meter. It i used in quite a number of Greek and Armenian folk tunes as well as some of today's pop tunes. Pink Floy had a major hit with their tune "Money" which is in 7/4. Yanni refers back to 7/8 quite a bit due to his Gree influence in his compositions. Rush had great success with their hit "Subdivisions" which switches betwee 4/4 and 7/8. Rush was probably one of the most influential and commercially successful when it came t incorporating odd time signatures in their compositions. And of course, last but not least, who could forge about Frank Zappa. Zappa would insert odd time bars in his compositions just to change things up ever now and again, as well as use them in whole compositions.

7/4 Examples

Let's look at some 7/4 examples. Example 9a is very simple, seven quarter notes to a measure. Look at th subdivisions though. This is the most common subdivision for 7/4 and 7/8. We have a 2+2+3 subdivision i example 9a. Now if we break the seven quarter notes down into eighth notes, we have example 9b. We ar still in a 2+2+3 subdivision. Examples 9c and 9d are two different ostinatos that we can come up with b combining the subdivisions from example 9b. Look at example 9c though, it has two dotted quarter note over the three grouping giving us the 2 over 3 feel that we are looking for. Example 9e is another way o subdividing 7/4. We could always flip the 2+2+3 subdivision around to give us a 3+2+2 but I figure you ca do that one on your own. Instead we'll do a 3+3+1 subdivision for 9e. This may seem a little strange but does work for medium to slow tempos. Example 9f is the ostinato based off of 9e, two dotted half note followed by a quarter note. If we break 9f down into eighth notes, we can subdivide the eighth notes int what we see in 9g, 3+3+3+3+2. Example 9h is another obstinato based off of the eighth notes in 9g. If w then break down the ostinato in 9h to sixteenth notes, we can subdivide the sixteenth notes into eight grou of three and a group of four. The ostinato that we get from that is in example 9j, eight dotted eighth note and a quarter note or two eighth notes. This may seem like a lot but it really isn't if you consider all the othe possibilities for 7/4. These are some of the more common subdivisions.

Here's what you need to practice before moving on to the 7/4 ideas. First let's set up a metronome or a drur machine to 80bpm. The click will be your quarter note. In 7/4 the quarter note is the largest commo denominator. If the click gets to be too much at first, turn it off until you learn these examples comfortabl Then practice them with the click. Instead of tapping example 9a with your foot, practice tapping example 9 instead. The reason for this is simple. By just counting out seven quarter notes with your foot, it's real eas to get lost in the count. By keeping example 9d in your foot, you will always be feeling that 2+2+3 ostinato n matter where you are in the bar. By doing this you can start to feel the 7/4 instead of having to count i When you get to the 3+3+1, tap the ostinato in 9f with your foot. This is for the same reason as we did fc the 2+2+3 subdivision. Practice tapping all these examples with both hands while keeping the ostinato i your foot. Be sure to give the dotted eighth notes and dotted quarter notes their full value. If you want to ge creative, try tapping some of the other ostinatos with your foot while clapping through these examples.

Good Luck!

7/4 Examples

7/4 Ideas

Okay, now that you've got the examples mastered, let's move on to some 7/4 ideas. Don't forget; learn thes[e] ideas first then try playing them with a click or a drum machine.

What better to start with than idea #1? Does it sound familiar? Idea #1 doesn't really have a subdivision to [it] other than just seven straight quarter notes to a measure with the second beat being a triplet figure. [I] included it though because it's a fairly well known bass line. Ideas #2 and #3 are based off of examples 9[c] and 9d, just a straight 2+2+3 ostinato. Idea #4 is an idea that can be used as a simple rock groove. It is st[ill] based off of a 2+2+3 subdivision, but it's just a straight eighth note groove. The main thing here is to be abl[e] to feel that 2+2+3 subdivision throughout all of these ideas so far with the exception of maybe idea #[1.] Those two dotted quarter notes in the 3 subdivision are very important to let the measures flow from one t[o] another without feeling much of a skip.

Ideas #5 and #6 are very similar in the fact that the subdivisions and the ostinato are identical but here i[s] where your choice of notes can change the whole style of the groove. Because #5 is a root-P5-octav[e] construction, it can be used in any type of a bossa nova or samba, but because #6 is a root-M3-P5-M[6] construction, it could be used in a blues shuffle. This is a great example of how your note choices ca[n] greatly change these ideas from one style to another. It's up to you to experiment with whatever style you'r[e] into and try out these ideas on that style.

Look at ideas #7, #8 and #9 these too can be used as a Latin or as a funk style just because of the not[e] choices. Try implementing the note choices from #6 and it can be used over a blues as well.

Another thing to practice is to try breaking down the ideas more rhythmically like I did in #7 and #8. Look a[t] the third and fourth bars in #7 and the second bar of #8. Little variations of the groove can keep the ide[as] from getting too monotonous

Ideas #10 and #11 are both based off of the 3+3+1 subdivision discussed at the end of the examples. Mak[e] sure to give each dotted quarter note it's full value.

Like I've said many times so far, It's all in how you play these ideas that will make the difference. These ar[e] only ideas, feel free to experiment with them and have some fun with them too.

7/4 Ideas

#1

#2

#3

#4

#5

#6

#7

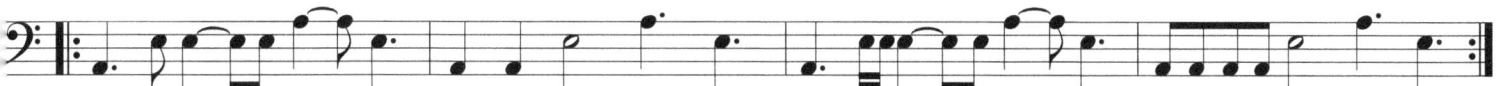

#8

#9

#10

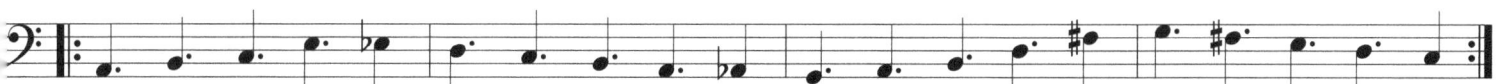

#11

7/8 Examples

The next section deals with 7/8. Again just like 7/4, you will notice a lot of the same subdivisions in 7/8 a[s] you did in 7/4. Remember though, 7/8 and 7/4 are two completely different time signatures. 7/4 has seve[n] quarter notes to a measure where 7/8 has seven eighth notes to a measure, which only comes out to b[e] three and a half quarter notes.

Let's look at example 10a. We have a 2+2+3 subdivision and like 7/4, this is the most common subdivisio[n] for 7/8. The ostinato that you can play is in example 10b, two quarter notes and a dotted quarter note. If w[e] break down the ostinato into sixteenth notes, we have what we see in example 10c, two groups of fou[r] sixteenth notes and two groups of three sixteenth notes. Pay attention to those two groups of three sixteent[h] notes! Example 10d is the ostinato we come up with from the sixteenth notes in example 10c. Its just lik[e] 10b only we have two dotted eighth notes in the end of the bar instead of a dotted quarter note. Example 10e and 10f are some variations of the previous four examples. Try to mix all the examples together b[y] taking different parts of each example and making your own examples.

Example 10g is the beginning of the second type of subdivision 3+3+1. This subdivision works with slo[w] tempos best. If it gets too fast, that last eighth note can get lost in the groove. Again, I could have just flippe[d] the subdivision around to be a 3+2+2 subdivision but I figured you could do that on your own. Example 10[h] is the ostinato based off of 10g, two dotted quarter notes and an eighth note. If we break that ostinato dow[n] into sixteenth notes, we come up with example 10i, four groups of three sixteenth notes and a group of tw[o] sixteenth notes. Example 10j is the ostinato that is based off of the sixteenth notes in example 10i, fou[r] dotted eighth notes followed by a single eighth note.

Here's what you need to practice before moving on to the 7/8 ideas. First let's set up a metronome or a drur[m] machine to 80bpm. The click will be your quarter note. In 7/8 the eighth note is the largest commo[n] denominator. If the click gets to be too much at first, turn it off until you learn these examples comfortabl[y] Then practice them with the click.
Like we did with 7/4, instead of having to keep seven quarter notes in our foot, let's keep the ostinato fro[m] 10b in our foot and practice tapping examples 10a through 10f. Then try the same thing with the ostinat[o] from 10 d in your foot.

When you get to the 3+3+1 subdivision, keep 10h in your foot while practicing 10g, 10h, 10i and 10j. I know [I] say this in for every time signature but it's real important to give those dotted eighth notes their full value[.] Even if you're not actually playing the sixteenth notes, you definitely should be feeling them or even singin[g] them.

See you in the 7/8 ideas!

7/8 Examples

10a

1 2 1 2 1 2 3

10b

1_2 1_2 1_2_3

10c

1 2 3 4 1 2 3 4 1 2 3 1 2 3

10d

1_2 1_2 1_2_3 1_2_3

10e

1 2 3_4 1 2 3_4 1 2 3 1 2 3

10f

1 2_3_4 1 2_3_4 1_2_3 1_2_3

10g

1 2 3 1 2 3 1

10h

1_2_3 1_2_3 1_2

10i

1 2 3 1 2 3 1 2 3 1 2 3 1 2

10j

1_2_3 1_2_3 1_2_3 1_2_3 1_2

7/8 Ideas

Let's look at some of these 7/8 ideas. Idea #1 is just your basic 2+2+3 subdivision but it works very well at any tempo. Be careful of those dotted eighth notes though. Idea #2 is based off of #1 only the first two quarter notes have been changed around a bit. Idea #3 is sort of a culmination of both #1 and #2 with a few other rhythmic figures put in. Practice this idea slowly at first. It's not as hard as it looks. These first three ideas work well as a samba due to their Root-P5-Octave construction. If we look at idea #4 though it is the exact same thing as #1 only my note choices are different, suited more towards a rock groove. Ideas #5 and #6 are some more rock grooves like #4. Be aware of the changing rhythmic figures in #6. Ideas #7 and #8 are a couple of funk ideas that you can use over 7/8. Again, it may look hard but once you get the 7/8 feeling good, it's not all that hard. All of the ideas in this section are in the 2+2+3 subdivision we discussed earlier. Idea #9 is no different except for the way it sounds compared to the other ideas. The note choices are pretty much the same but listen to the way it's played! The bonus idea is something that could be played over any 7/8 groove. Don't spend a whole lot of time trying to read it though. This is to just give you idea of what can be played without using the same idea over and over, while sticking to the same subdivision and the same style.

Remember that these ideas are merely just ideas. As long as you have the basic knowledge of what notes to use for different styles, you can apply that knowledge to these ideas. For instance, a walking blues could easily be implied over ideas #1 or #4 just by playing the Root-M3-P5-m7 of whatever dominant chord you're using. By knowing that most country bass lines consist of a Root-P5 below construction, you turn a simple country bass line into a cool 7/8 groove. Use your imagination to come up with different ideas of your own.

7/8 Ideas

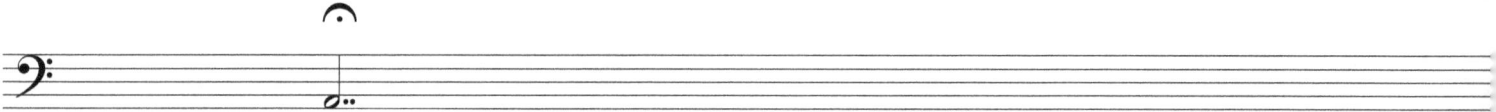

7/4 & 7/8 Chart

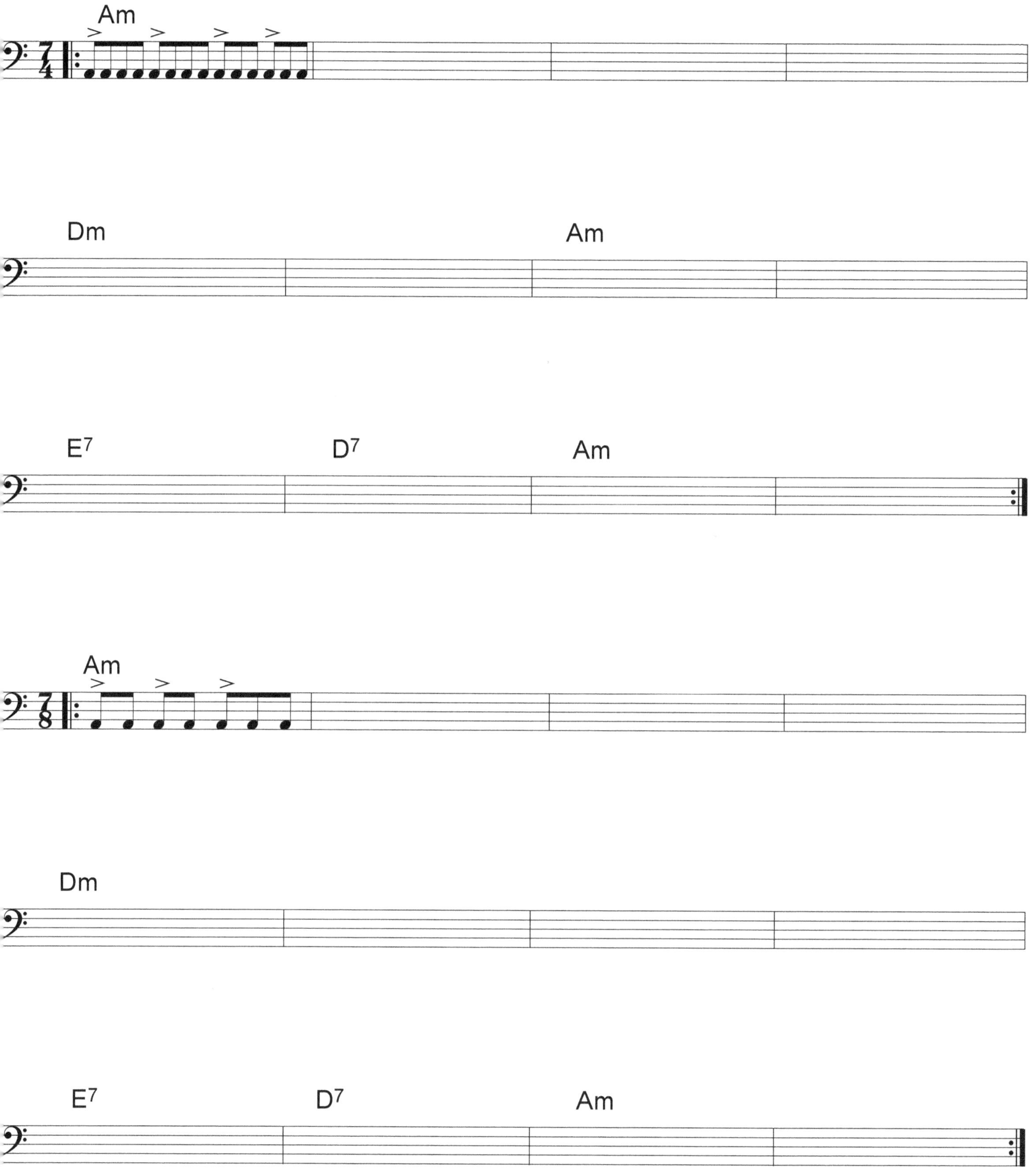

You are probably wondering why we're only covering 9/8 in this chapter and not 9/4. We did it with all the other time signatures by covering the eighth note as well as the quarter note. The reason for this is when the meters start getting larger and larger, staying with the quarter note starts to let the measures get too long. Could you imagine a signature of 15/4 with 15 quarter notes to a bar. That would mean that the drummer providing he or she were playing eighth notes on the hi-hat or ride, would have to play thirty, eighth notes for each bar. The phrases just get to be too long when dealing with the quarter note. 7/4 seems to be the cut of for quarter note meters. This doesn't mean that there is no such thing as 9/4 or 11/4, there certainly is, it's just not all that common.

9/8 is another triple meter just like three's, six's and twelve's like we discussed in an earlier chapter. It i based off of three groups of thrEe eighth notes. The difference between 9/8 and all the other triple meters i that it works just as well being subdivided into a 2+3 combination also. For instance, you could use 2+2+2+3 subdivision as well as a 3+3+3 subdivision. You can't do that with the other triple meters becaus they are all even numbers except for 3/4 and 3/8 which can only have a three grouping because of the small meters.

9/8 Examples

Let's look at some 9/8 examples. Example 11a is one of the two most common subdivisions for 9/8, a 3+3+ subdivision. Example 11b is the ostinato we come up with from example 11a. Three dotted eighth notes. we break example 11b down into sixteenth notes, we can group them into six groups of three like we have i example 11c. Example 11d is the ostinato that we come up with from 11c. Six dotted eighth notes. Now, let' look at examples 11e and 11f. They are the same as 11a and 11b, the only difference being the two dotte eighth not☐es at the end of the bar. I put these last because you need to work on 11c's sixteenth note groups of three before you go on to the dotted eighth notes in 11e and 11f.

Example 11g is the next subdivision for 9/8 it is grouped into a 2+2+3 subdivision. The ostinato(s) we com up with are in examples 11h and 11i. By breaking 11g down into sixteenth notes we can then group them like we have in example 11j, three groups of four and two groups of three, and example 11l, four groups c three, a group of four, and a group of two. The ostinatos for each of these sixteenth note groupings are i examples 11k and 11m. Example 11k's group of two dotted eighth notes can also be used in in 11h and 1 in place of the dotted eighth note.

Okay, this seems like a lot. That's because there's a lot that you can do with 9/8.
Here's what you need to practice before moving on to the 9/8 ideas. First let's set up a metronome or a drur machine to 80bpm. The click will be your eighth note. In 9/8 the eighth note is the largest commo denominator. If the click gets to be too much at first, turn it off until you learn these examples comfortabl Then practice them with the click.

For the first subdivision, practice tapping example 11b with your foot while tapping examples 11a throug 11f with your hands. Be sure to get all the accent markings right. Even in the ostinatos, you should still b feeling those sixteenth note groupings. When you get to the 2+2+3 subdivision, practice tapping example 11g through 11k while tapping 11h in your foot. Make sure to accent all the accent markings. Examples 1 and 11m are extras. Feel free to work on them if you have time. Try practicing 11l with your hands whil tapping 11m with your feet.

Good luck and I'll see you over in the ideas.

9/8 Examples

11a

1 2 3 1 2 3 1 2 3

11b

1_2_3 1_2_3 1_2_3

11c

1 2 3 1 2 3 1 2 3 1 2 3 1 2 3 1 2 3

11d

1_2_3 1_2_3 1_2_3 1_2_3 1_2_3 1_2_3

11e

1 2 3 1 2 3 1_2_3 1_2_3

11f

1_2_3 1_2_3 1_2_3 1_2_3

11g

1 2 1 2 1 2 1 2 3

11h

1_2 1_2 1_2 1_2_3

11i

1+2+3+ 57 1_2_3

58

9/8 Ideas

#1

#2

#3

#4

#5

#6

#7

#8

#9

#10

#11

#12

9/8 Ideas

Congratulations on getting through the 9/8 examples. In this section we'll look at some different ideas for bass lines based off of both the 3+3+3 subdivision and the 2+2+2+3 subdivision. To keep things simple, most of these ideas are done over an A minor vamp. Ideas #1, 2 and 3 are based on a II-V-I chord progression to show a jazz walking line and ideas #10, 11 and 12 are done over an E minor vamp to show a funk line.

Idea #1 is based off of the three groups of three eighth notes tied into three dotted quarter notes. Notice how the line outlines the chord tones of the chord to simulate a walking bass line. Idea #2 two is the same walking line only it's done over the 2+2+3 subdivision. Idea #3 is just another version of #2 only the three quarter notes are tied into a dotted half note. Idea #4 is an eighth note groove based off of the 2+2+3 subdivision. Idea #5 is another way of playing the 3+3+3 subdivision with the dotted eighth notes at the front of the bar. Idea #6 is just a straight ahead eighth note groove based off of the 3+3+3 subdivision. Ideas #4, 5 and 6 can be used as rock grooves or even as ska grooves providing you've got your right hand muting technique down. Ideas #7, 8 and 9 are all from the 2+2+3 subdivision and can be used as different Latin grooves such as a samba. This is due to the Root-P5-Octave construction. Ideas #10, 11 and 12 are all different variations of a funk groove over an E minor vamp. They are all based off of the 3+3+3 subdivision.

Practice all of these ideas slowly at first and remember just because some of these ideas are listed as a certain style, it doesn't mean that they can't be interpreted into other styles as well. For instance, idea #1 doesn't necessarily have to be used as a walking jazz line. Try using it as a rock line or a Latin line. Like I said earlier, it's all in how YOU play them and the notes you choose. Here's something else to practice. Try mixing up the ideas. For instance, try playing three bars of let's say idea #4 and on the last bar, use one measure of idea #5 as a turnaround. This can lead to a whole new slew of ideas for you.

Good Luck!!!

9/8 Chart

Chapter 8, 11/8

In this chapter we'll look at some different 11/8 subdivisions and ideas. Like I said in chapter 7, we won't g into 11/4 because of the length of the phrases. 11/8 can be looked at as a combination of different mete such as a combination of seven and four or visa versa. It could also be looked at as a combination of six an five. Let's look at some of the examples!

11/8 Examples

Example 12a is the first grouping that we'll discuss, 2+2+2+2+3, four groups of two, and a group of three You can also think of it as four and seven. Another way of thinking of it would be a bar of 4/4 and a bar 3/8. You can actually count out four quarter notes and then three eighth notes. Notice how the bar is divided Example 12b is the ostinato that we come up with from example 12a, four quarter notes and a dotted quarte note. If we break example 12b into sixteenth notes, we come up with the groupings in example 12c, fou groups of four and two groups of three. The ostinato in example 12d is pretty close to that in 12b, the on difference being the dotted eighth notes at the end of the bar instead of the dotted quarter note. This because of the two groups of three sixteenth notes in example 12c.

The next four examples are based off of another subdivision. Example 12e is a 3+3+3+2 subdivision, thre groups of three and a group of two, or six and five. Example 12f is the ostinato based off of that subdivision If we break example 12f into sixteenth notes, we can then group them into six groups of three and a group four like we have in example 12g. The ostinato in 12h is what we come up with from 12g, six dotted eight notes and a quarter note.

Example 12i is another subdivision based off of example 12a. This time it's turned around as a 2+2+3+2+ subdivision. Be sure to accent the down beat of the bar because it's easy to turn it around into example 12 if you're not paying attention. Example 12j is the ostinato we get from 12i.

Here's what you need to practice before moving on to the 11/8 ideas. First let's set up a metronome or drum machine to 80bpm. The click will be your eighth note. In 11/8 the eighth note is the largest commo denominator. If the click gets to be too much at first, turn it off until you learn these examples comfortabl Then practice them with the click.
For the first subdivision, practice tapping examples 12a through 12d with your hands while keeping th ostinato from 12b with your foot. Then practice the same thing only with the ostinato from 12d in your foot.
When you get to the next subdivision in 12e, practice tapping examples 12e through 12h with your hand while tapping the ostinato from 12f with your foot.
Examples 12i and 12j are simple practice tapping 12i with your hands while tapping 12j with your foot. Yo can use the same sixteenth note ostinato from example 12d, just make sure to have it subdivided like 12i.

Good Luck and I'll see you in the 11/8 ideas!

11/8 Examples

12a

1 2 1 2 1 2 1 2 1 2 3

12b

1_2 1_2 1_2 1_2 1_2_3

12c

1 e + a 2 e + a 3 e + a 4 e + a 1 2 3 1 2 3

12d

1e+a 2e+a 3e+a 4e+a 1_2_3 1_2_3

12e

1 2 3 1 2 3 1 2 3 1 2

12f

1_2_3 1_2_3 1_2_3 1_2

12g

1 2 3 1 2 3 1 2 3 1 2 3 1 2 3 1 2 3 1 2

12h

1_2_3 1_2_3 1_2_3 1_2_3 1_2_3 1_2_3 1e+a

12i

1 2 1 2 1 2 3 1 2 1 2

12j

1_2 1_2 1_2_3 1_2_3 1_2 1_2

11/8 Ideas

Welcome to the 11/8 ideas! In this section we'll look at some ideas that we can use based on the 11/8 examples that we discussed in the previous section. To make things easier, most of these ideas are taken from a one chord vamp in A minor. Ideas #10, 11 and 12 are taken from a one chord vamp in E minor.

Let's take a look at idea #1. It is based on the 2+2+3+2+2 subdivision from example 12i with the two dotted eighth notes in the middle of the phrase. This particular idea would work well over a Latin groove such as samba. Again, this is only because of the notes I've chosen to play. Try outlining an A minor arpeggio with the same subdivision and it could turn into a minor blues idea. Idea #2 is another variation of idea #1 only with two quarter notes at the end of the bar instead of four quarter notes. Idea #3 is yet another variation of idea #1. The difference here is that the sixteenth note figures give more of a samba feel. Be careful though, the first two groups are dotted eighth-sixteenth note groupings whereas the second two groups are just an eighth-sixteenth note grouping. Ideas #4 and #5 are some basic quarter note and eighth note ideas that can be used for different rock grooves. These are based off of the 2+2+2+2+3 subdivision in example 12a. Ideas #6, 7, 8 and 9 are all taken from the 3+3+3+2 subdivisions in example 12e. These are pretty generic and can be used for just about any type of groove. Try incorporating them into whatever style you like. Idea #9 works especially well as a turn around at the end of let's say a four bar phrase. Try playing any of these ideas and on the fourth bar use idea #9 as a turn around. I think you'll be surprised at how well it works. Ideas #10, 11 and 12 are some funk ideas in E minor that you can work on. These ideas are taken from the 2+2+2+2+3 subdivision again. This subdivision works well with a funk line because you can actually incorporate your 4/4 ideas into this because of the four groups of eighth notes followed by the two dotted eighth or a single quarter note.

11/8 Ideas

#1

#2

#3

#4

#5

#6

#7

#8

#9

#10

#11

#12

11/8 Chart

Chapter 9, Multiple Meter Charts

One of the most difficult things about playing in odd meters is being able to play from one time signature t[o] another without missing a beat. So far we've learned how to play in a number of different meters. Now wha[t] happens if we were to combine some of those different meters in a song? This is where it gets tricky. Thi[s] chapter will help you deal with being able to play multiple meters within a chart. What you learn in thi[s] chapter applies to all meters, even going from a bar of 4/4 to a bar of 2/4 which is quite common in som[e] songs.

Let's look at Multi-Meter Chart #1. It may look pretty intimidating but it's not as hard as it looks. First lets se[t] up a metronome to about 160bpm. This may sound fast but remember, the click is going to be the eight[h] note. Even though we have a chart that goes from 4/4 to 7/8 to 9/8 to 3/8 to 7/8, the largest commo[n] denominator between all these meters is the eighth note. This means that the eighth note will remai[n] constant throughout the entire chart. Going from one time signature to another will not affect the eighth note[.] It should remain constant. Remember, there's no special tricks here, that eighth note will be the sam[e] whether you're in 4/4, 7/8, 3/8, or 9/8.
The subdivisions have been added at the beginning of each time signature to let you know what to pla[y] throughout the piece. I added a style reference at the top of each part to give you an idea as to what style t[o] play with on the CD. Before playing along with the CD, try clapping the rhythms through the piece firs[t.] When you get comfortable with the rhythms, try playing along with the CD.

Now let's look at Multi-Meter Chart #2. This chart has more of a twelve bar blues chord progression to it. Yo[u] have four bars of 3/4 to to bars of 5/4 back to two bars of 3/4 to four bars of 11/8. Because of the 11/8, th[e] eighth note is the largest common denominator throughout this piece. The eighth note will remain constar[nt] through the entire chart RIGHT? The subdivisions are added at the start of each time signature. Again, tr[y] clapping out the entire chart before trying it on the bass. When you feel comfortable with it, move on t[o] playing it with the CD. I left the styles out because I want you to add your own stylistic preferences to th[e] chart. Just because it's a blues chord progression doesn't mean it has to be a blues song.

Multi-Meter Chart #3 is yet another conglomeration of time changes. We've got four bars of 9/8 to four bar[s] of 7/8, to four bars of 5/4. Guess what the largest common denominator is between all the time changes? [If] you said the eighth note again, you're right. Again, I left out the styles so use your own. I did leave in th[e] subdivisions though. Practice clapping through it and then go ahead and play it with the CD

Multi-Meter Chart #1

Funk

Latin

Funk

Swing

Funk

Multi-Meter Chart #2

Multi-Meter Chart #3

Chapter 10, Playing Over the Barline

There is one last thing that I would like to cover. So far throughout this book we have covered the mos[t] popular odd time signatures all of which can be used to anyone's advantage in composing music and/or jus[t] playing some cool grooves. Everything that we've covered so far though relates to what are called one ba[r] phrases. Meaning that the same rhythmic phrase repeats from one bar to the next, over, and over. Whil[e] this is always useful, sometimes it can get monotonous. One way to cure this was discussed briefly in a fe[w] of the chapters by playing a rhythmic phrase for three bars and then playing a turnaround in the fourth bar[.] This always works well because it gives the impression of a four bar phrase. Just as a drummer m[]ight pla[y] the same beat for four bars and then at the end of the fourth bar, add a crash on the cymbal to designate th[e] end of a four bar phrase.

Another way might be to play the same phrase from measure to measure only every other measure addin[g] a rest(s) where there might have been a note(s) played in the previous measure, this giving your two ba[r] phrase more space.

The other way to add some "spice" to your phrases is to do what's called playing over the barline. No, [it] doesn't mean hopping up on the bar and playing from where the bartender stands. What it does mean i[s] this, instead of playing the "one" or down beat of each bar, try skipping over it from one measure to the nex[t.] This will really give you and the listener the feeling of a two bar phrase. Our natural instinct is to play th[e] downbeat of each measure to let us and everyone listening know exactly where the "one" is for ever[y] measure. In most Western music, this is the norm. James Brown made a whole career out of nailing the on[e] each and every bar. In some cultures and music though, that isn't so. In the words of the great percussionis[t] Efrain Toro "THOSE DAMN BARLINES!"

Did you ever wonder how a drummer can get completely away from playing the "one" but yet still kno[w] exactly where he or she is in the measure?

Here's how!
Let's look at some of these Over The Barline examples. The 5/8 example shows a simple 3+2 subdivision[.] The next example after that shows the sixteenth note breakdown from the eighth notes. Now, if we take the[e] sixteenth note example and just play the upbeats of the sixteenth notes, we have what's in the thir[d] example, just the upbeats. Now we can carry those upbeats from measure to measure without having t[o] land on the "one" unless we want to. The last two measures are a two bar phrase that might give you som[e] ideas.
The 7/8 examples are the same ideas as 5/8 only over 7/8 which would add two more upbeats to you[r] phrase. Notice the two-bar phrase at the bottom
When dealing with quarter note meters such as the 5/4 examples, you can use either the upbeats on th[e] eighth notes or the upbeats on the sixteenth notes.
Try practicing clapping these examples going from the sixteenth notes and eighth notes to just the upbeats[.] Do this while tapping the ostinato with your foot. This may not come very easily at first but with a littl[e] practice, it will come. I remember having a hard time with it because I was so use to playing just downbeat[s] at first. What I did was I would play the downbeats with my right hand into a pillow so all I could hear wer[e] the upbeats. This at least let me hear what it was supposed to sound like. The main idea here is to FEEL th[e] upbeats as well as the downbeats.

5/8 Over The Barline

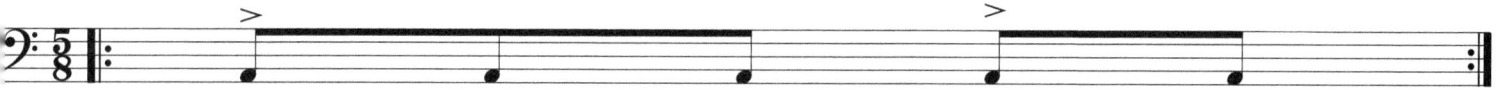

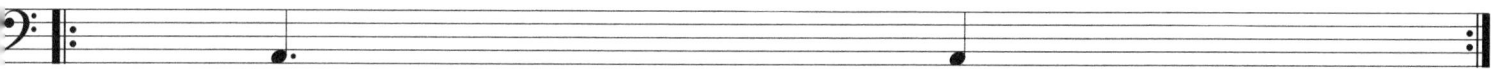

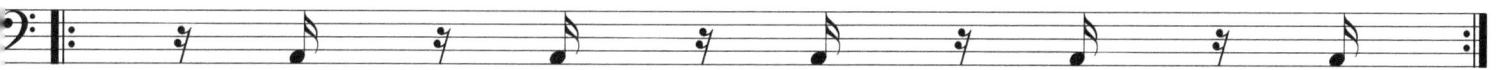

7/8 Over The Barline

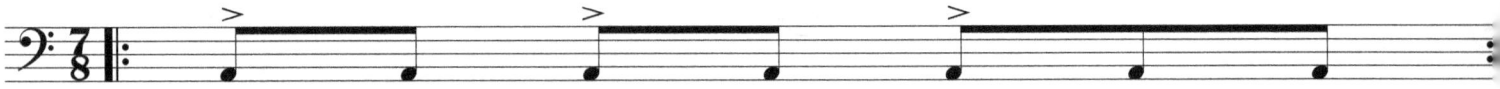

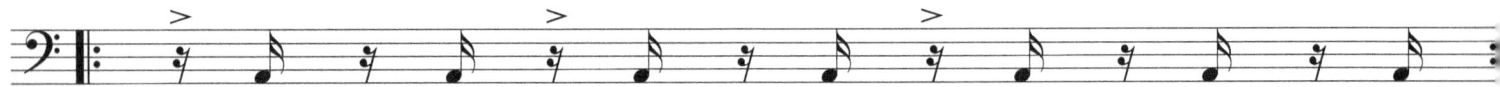

1	Tuning Note	1:09
2	2/3 Subdivision	0:32
3	3/4 Ideas 1 - 14	2:40
4	3/8 Ideas 1 - 7	2:19
5	3/4 Chart	1:01
6	3/8 Chart	0:49
7	6/4 Ideas 1 - 3	1:22
8	6/4 Ideas 4 - 5	0:47
9	6/4 Ideas 6 - 8	1:27
10	6/4 Ideas 9 - 11	1:20
11	6/8 Ideas 1 - 5	1:44
12	6/8 Ideas 6 - 9	1:12
13	6/8 Ideas 10 - 12	1:00
14	6/4 Chart	1:07
15	6/8 Chart	1:03
16	12/8 Ideas 1 - 5	1:40
17	12/8 Ideas 6 - 7	1:00
18	12/8 Ideas 8 - 9	1:02
19	12/8 Ideas 10 - 12	1:16
20	12/8 Ideas 13 - 14	0:57
21	12/8 Chart	1:28
22	5/4 Ideas 1 - 5	1:35
23	5/4 Ideas 6 - 8	1:06
24	5/4 Ideas 9 - 10	1:04
25	5/4 Ideas Bonus	0:37
26	5/8 Ideas 1 - 9	2:00
27	5/4 Chart	1:13
28	5/8 Chart	0:48
29	7/4 Ideas 1 - 4	1:57
30	7/4 Ideas 5 - 6	1:02
31	7/4 Ideas 7 - 9	1:26
32	7/4 Ideas 10 - 11	0:57
33	7/8 Ideas 1 - 6	1:48
34	7/8 Ideas 7 - 9	1:09
35	7/8 Ideas Bonus	0:44
36	7/4 Chart	1:48
37	7/8 Chart	1:03
38	9/8 Ideas 1 - 3	0:48
39	9/8 Ideas 4 - 6	1:08
40	9/8 Ideas 7 - 9	1:25
41	9/8 Ideas 10 - 12	1:09
42	9/8 Chart	1:08
43	11/8 Ideas 1 - 5	1:55

44	11/8 Ideas 6 - 9	1:28
45	11/8 Ideas 10 - 12	1:34
46	11/8 Chart	1:27
47	Multi Meter Chart 1	1:03
48	Multi Meter Chart 2	1:45
49	Multi Meter Chart 3	1:15